W9-CAG-449

Sight Words and Vocabulary

This book belongs to

_____

© Disney/Pixar, Mazda Miata®

Bendon, Inc. Ashland, OH 44805

Copyright © 2020 by Disney Enterprises, Inc./Pixar All rights reserved.
No part of this book may be reproduced or transmitted in any form or by any means,
electronic or mechanical, including photocopying, recording, or by any information storage
and retrieval system, without written permission from the publisher.

Materials and characters from the movie *Cars*. Copyright © 2006, 2010 Disney Enterprises, Inc./Pixar.
Disney/Pixar elements ©Disney/Pixar, not including underlying vehicles owned by third parties; and, if applicable:
Chevrolet and H-1 Hummer are trademarks of General Motors; Dodge, Hudson Hornet, Plymouth Superbird are
trademarks of Chrysler LLC; Fiat is a trademark of Fiat S.p.A.; Mack is a registered trademark of Mack Trucks, Inc.;
Mazda Miata is a registered trademark of Mazda Motor Corporation; Mercury and Model T are registered
trademarks of Ford Motor Company; Petty marks used by permission of Petty Marketing LLC; Porsche is
a trademark of Porsche; Sarge's rank insignia design used with the approval of the U.S. Army; Volkswagen
trademarks, design patents and copyrights are used with the approval of the owner Volkswagen AG.

Visit www.disneybooks.com

CONSULTANTS:
Alice Dickstein, Reading and Language Arts, New York, NY
Linda Vahey, Mathematics, Medfield, MA
Beth Sycamore, Reading and Mathematics, Chicago, IL

Editorial Development by Brown Publishing Network, Inc. Waltham, MA 02453
Design by Sequel Creative, Fairfield, CT

If you purchased this book without a cover, you should be aware that this book is stolen property. It was reported as "unsold
and destroyed" to the publisher, and neither the author nor the publisher has received payment for this "stripped" book.

Dear Parent,

School Skills Workbooks are the perfect tools to make a difference in your child's learning. Inside this book you'll find a developmental progression of activities designed to help your child master essential skills critical for school success. Interactive stickers, games, flash cards, and more will help your child review, practice, and master more than fifty of the most common concept and high-frequency words.

In order to become proficient readers and writers, children must be able to quickly recognize a core group of high-frequency words. These words are used over and over again in books, and many of them are not spelled the way they sound. Repeated opportunities for children to talk about these words, point to letters that make up these words, and use these words in a variety of ways help them build an efficient sight-word vocabulary.

As partners in learning with **School Skills Workbooks**, you can help your child reach important milestones to become a confident and independent learner.

Disney/Pixar, Chevrolet®, Fiat™, Hudson Hornet™, Jeep®, ©Volkswagen AG

Let's Learn Sight Words and Vocabulary

How fast can you read this word: *and*? You'll find this word over and over again when you read. Words you see a lot are important to know. This book will help you practice reading and writing words. And, you'll find stickers, games, and flash cards to make learning these words lots of fun.

These 14 words make up most of the words you read and write.

a

and

for

he

is

in

she

you

the

it

was

to

that

of

4

© Disney/Pixar

Some words go together because of what they mean. Color words are like that.

yellow

blue

red

Look for letters you know in words. Count how many letters in each word. Count them low and slow!

up

there

came

Read lots of books that aren't too hard or too easy. Read them again and again!

© Disney/Pixar, Fiat™, Porsche®, ©Volkswagen AG

Lightning McQueen, racing superstar number 95, has set up headquarters in Radiator Springs. Lightning loves the little town and has made lots of good friends.

But setting up his headquarters in Radiator Springs is just the beginning. Lightning has a fantastic idea that will make the town as super famous as he is!

© Disney/Pixar; Fiat™, Hudson Hornet™, Jeep®; Sarge's rank insignia design used with the approval of the U.S. Army, Mercury™, Model T™, Porsche®, ©Volkswagen AG

"Listen up, everybody," Lightning says. "Let's have a car rally right here in Radiator Springs! Every car in the country will want to be part of the fun and excitement! What do you think, folks?"

At first, all the cars just stared at Lightning. His words took a minute to sink in. Then everyone shouted, "A car rally here in Radiator Springs! What a super idea!"

© Disney/Pixar, Chevrolet®, Hudson Hornet™, Mack®, ©Volkswagen AG

Lightning calls up reporters from TV stations and newspapers. He tells them he has a BIG news story.

Lightning says to himself: "Radiator Springs is going to be the place where big things happen!"

© Disney/Pixar

The reporters arrive quickly. Cameras are turned on and lights flash. Lightning speaks into the microphones. "Radiator Springs will hold its first-ever car rally one week from Saturday! It will be the best rally ever, and we hope to see cars from every city and town!"

"What a terrific idea!" exclaim the reporters.

"You bet!" agrees Lightning. "Ka-chow!"

© Disney/Pixar, Mack®, Porsche®, ©Volkswagen AG

Let's Learn Words for Feelings

How do the cars feel about Lightning's idea? Let's see!

happy

Doc is happy.

scared

Red is scared.
He doesn't like crowds.

excited

Mater is excited.

© Disney/Pixar, Hudson Hornet™

surprised

Luigi is surprised.
"Mama mia!" he keeps saying.

worried

Sally is worried.
There is so much work to do!

mad

Chick is mad that he didn't
think of the idea!

sad

Nobody is sad!

© Disney/Pixar, Fiat™, Hudson Hornet™, Jeep®, Porsche®, ©Volkswagen AG

Let's Match Words

Read each feelings word. Find the matching sticker on page 81.

happy

mad

scared

feelings

worried

excited

surprised

© Disney/Pixar. Fiat™, Hudson Hornet™, Porsche®

Let's Sort Words

Read each word.
Count the letters in each word.
Write the words in the chart.

said	so	but	is

2 letters	3 letters	4 letters

Write the missing word. Use a word from the chart.

_____
_____
_____ happy.

© Disney/Pixar, Fiat™, Hudson Hornet™

Let's Write Words

Read the words.
Write the missing word to complete each sentence.

There	has	of	from

1. 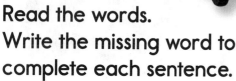 _____ a good idea.

2. But he has a lot _____ work to do.

3. 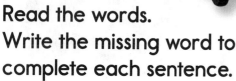 gets help _____ his friends.

4. _____ are many jobs to do.

© Disney/Pixar, Chevrolet®, Fiat™, Model T™, ©Volkswagen AG

Look at each car.
Circle the word that
tells how the car feels.

   sad   happy

   excited   sad

   happy   mad

Draw how you feel when you get a new toy.

© Disney/Pixar. Hudson Hornet™

Let's Learn Words for Days of the Week

Lightning and his pals have only one week to get ready for the rally. There is so much to do!

"Let's make a list," says Lightning. "We'll do one job each day!"

Sunday

Pave.

Monday

Wash.

Thursday

Get tires.

Friday

Get gas.

© Disney/Pixar, Chevrolet®, Fiat™, Hudson Hornet™, Jeep®, Mercury™, Porsche®, ©Volkswagen AG

Tuesday

Clean.

Wednesday

Paint.

Saturday

Make signs.

© Disney/Pixar, Chevrolet®, Fiat™

Let's Review Words for Days of the Week

Look at Lightning's calendar.

Sunday
Pave.

Monday
Wash.

Tuesday
Clean.

Wednesday
Paint.

Thursday
Get tires.

Friday
Get gas.

Saturday
Make signs.

Circle the correct day of the week.

Sunday   Monday

Tuesday   Thursday

Friday   Saturday

Monday   Wednesday

18

© Disney/Pixar. Chevrolet®, Fiat™, Hudson Hornet™, Mercury™

Let's Sort Words

Read each word.
Count the letters in each word.
Write the words in the chart.

the	do	they	on

2 letters	3 letters	4 letters

Write the missing word. Use a word from the chart.

_____ cars need .

© Disney/Pixar, Porsche®

Let's Write Words

Read the words.
Write the missing word to complete each sentence.

and   That   All   have

1. The  _____

_____

_____ so much work!

2. _____

_____ the  work.

3. The  clean _____

_____ clean.

4. _____

_____ is not clean.

© Disney/Pixar, Chevrolet®, Fiat™, Jeep®, Mercury™

Let's Find Words

Help Sally find Lightning.
Follow the words for the days of the week.

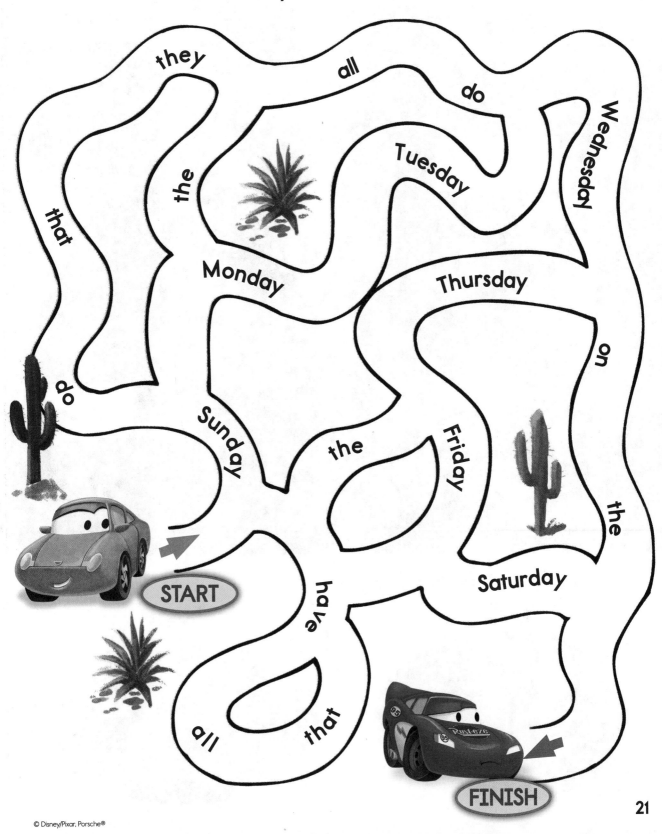

© Disney/Pixar. Porsche®

Let's Learn Words for Things in a Neighborhood

Lightning and his pals fix up their town. Radiator Springs looks better than ever.

firehouse

sign

store

street

Can you find these things?

store

firehouse

© Disney/Pixar, Fiat™, Hudson Hornet™

When visitors come for the rally,
they will see a very busy Main Street.

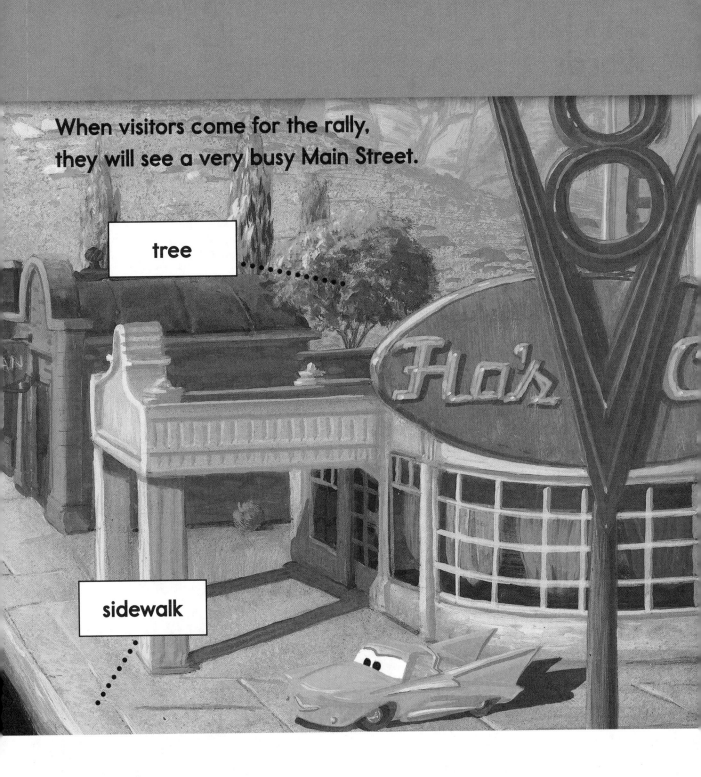

tree

sidewalk

sign

tree

© Disney/Pixar

Let's Match Words

Read each question.
Find the correct answer sticker
on page 81.

1. Who works in a store?

2. Who works on the street?

3. Who works in a firehouse?

Draw something you buy in a food store.

© Disney/Pixar, Fiat™

Let's Write Words

Read the words.
Write the missing word to complete each sentence.

> a   in   go   are

1. There _____ many in town.

2. _____ on the streets.

3. works in _____ store.

4. lives _____ the firehouse.

© Disney/Pixar, Chevrolet®, Fiat™, Jeep®; Sarge's rank insignia design used with the approval of the U.S. Army, Mercury™, Porsche®, ©Volkswagen AG

Let's Sort Words

Look at the pictures and words.
Write the words in the chart.

fire hose　　**oil cans**　　**tires**　　**firefighter**

Things you see in a store	Things you see in a firehouse
_____	_____
- - - - - - - - - - - - -	- - - - - - - - - - - - -
_____	_____
_____	_____
- - - - - - - - - - - - -	- - - - - - - - - - - - -
_____	_____

Draw a picture of your favorite store.

© Disney/Pixar

Flash Card Directions:

Cut out the flash cards. Have your child read each flash card one at a time. Help your child think of ways to sort the words. *For example:* sort the words by those that have the same beginning letter or number of letters.

all	and	are	do
go	has	have	in
is	of	on	said
a	that	the	they
but	there	from	so

Let's Review Word Meanings

Read each sentence.
Put a ✓ under **Yes** or **No**.

	Yes	No
1. I can walk in a tree.	☐	☐
2. I can walk on a sign.	☐	☐
3. I can walk in a store.	☐	☐

Draw a picture of a sign in your neighborhood.

© Disney/Pixar, Chevrolet®, Fiat™, Jeep®; Sarge's rank insignia used with the approval of the U.S. Army, Model T™, Porsche®, ©Volkswagen AG

Everyone in town works hard. They are busy from morning until night.

This morning, Red is washing store windows. But when he looks up at the sky, he gets scared! "What's happening?" cries Red. "The sky is so dark!"

Red races off to find Sheriff.

30

© Disney/Pixar

Sheriff asks Al Oft, the blimp,
to look around from up high.
"Don't worry, Red," says
Sheriff. "Al will find out why
the sky is so dark."

The cars wait. Soon Al Oft comes back
and reports, "I see a tornado out there!
It may be coming our way!"

"Oh, no!" groan the cars. "If a tornado hits,
we'll have to call off the car rally!"

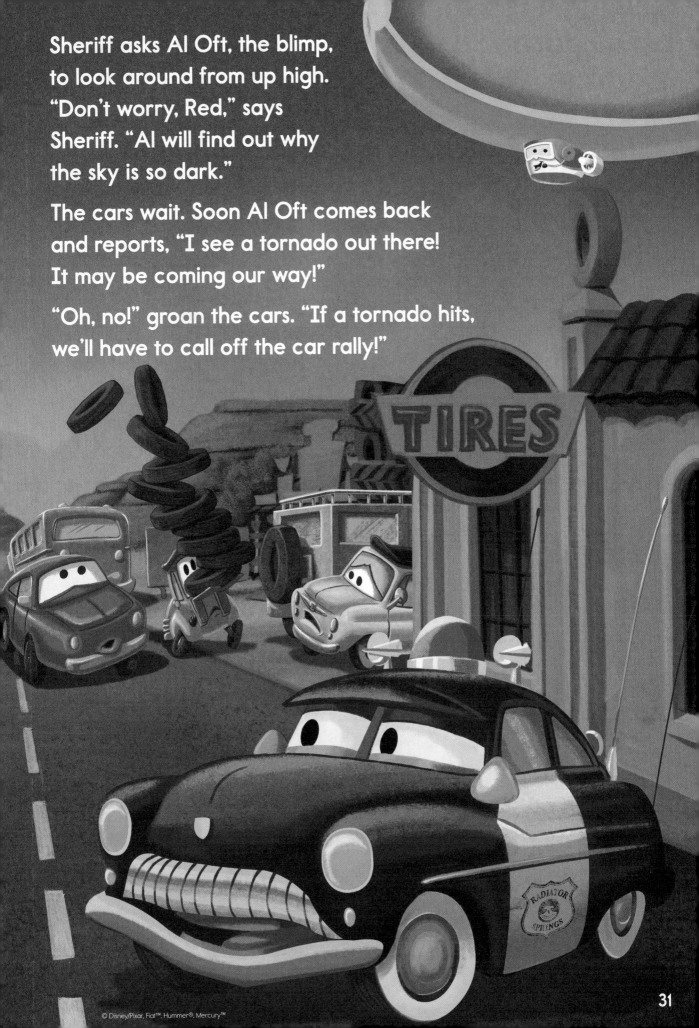

© Disney/Pixar, Fiat™, Hummer®, Mercury™

Let's Learn Weather Words

The tornado is heading toward
Radiator Springs!
The sun is not shining, and there
is a lot of wind blowing.
There is no rain, but there are
big dark clouds in the sky.

clouds

tornado

wind

© Disney/Pixar

Let's Match Words

Read each weather word.
Find the matching sticker
on page 81.

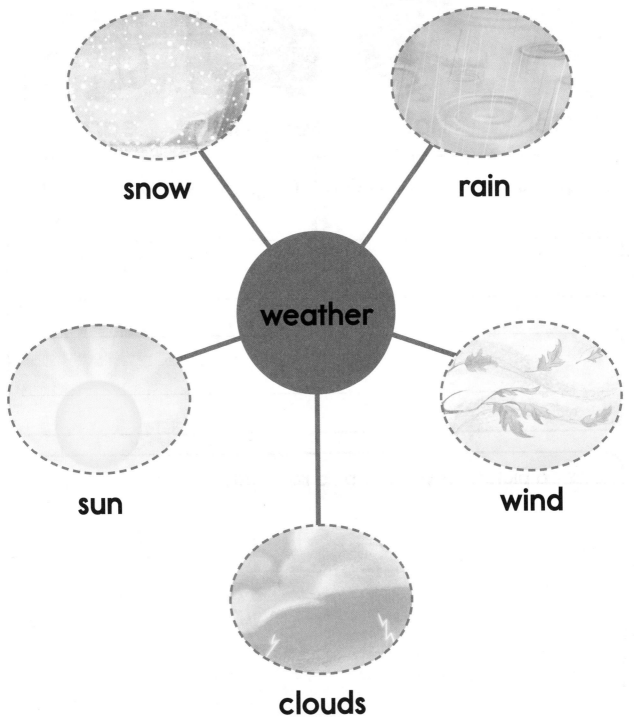

snow

rain

weather

sun

wind

clouds

© Disney/Pixar, Chevrolet®, Hudson Hornet™

Let's Sort Words

Look at the pictures and words.
Write the words in the chart

water   **hat**    **sunglasses**    **earmuffs**

Things cars need on a snowy day.	Things cars need on a sunny day.

Draw a picture of yourself on a rainy day.

34

© Disney/Pixar, Porsche®

Let's Sort Words

Read each word.
Count the letters in each word.
Write the words in the chart.

came	got	their	were

3 letters	4 letters	5 letters

Write the missing word. Use a word from the chart.

The cars _____ scared.

© Disney/Pixar

Let's Write Words

Read the words.
Write the missing word to
complete each sentence.

one   went   to   was

1. _____

   _____ up in the sky.

2. A _____

     _____ coming!

3. The  didn't want the _____
   ---- ----
   _____ come.

4. No _____

      _____ was happy about the .

36

© Disney/Pixar, Fiat™, Jeep®, Mercury™

Let's Find Words

Help Al Oft get back to his friends.
Follow the weather words.

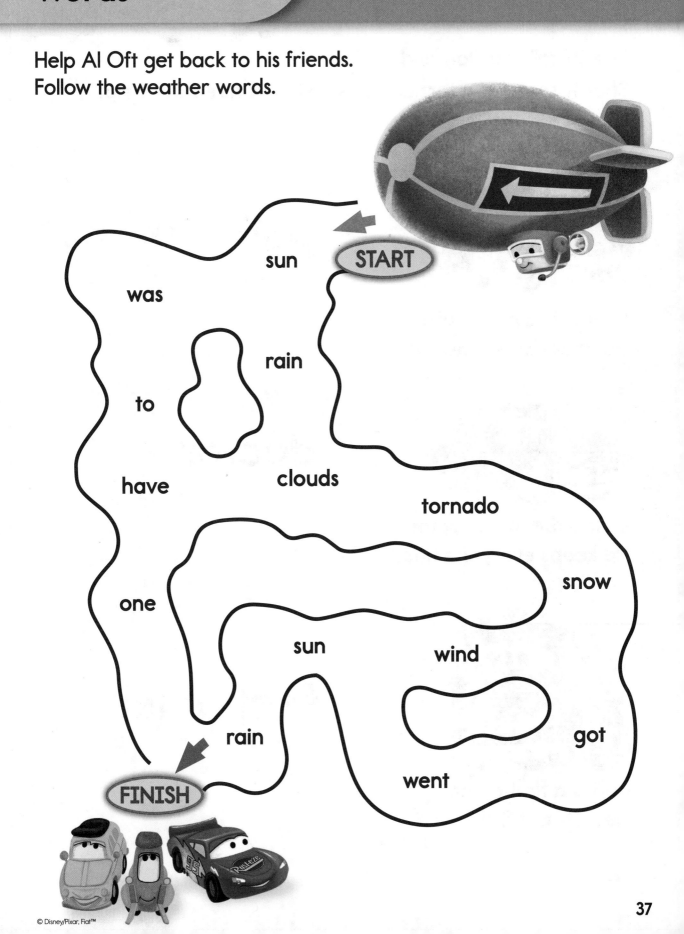

START

sun

was

rain

to

have

clouds

tornado

snow

one

sun

wind

got

rain

went

FINISH

© Disney/Pixar, Fiat™

Let's Learn Words for Neighborhood Helpers

Sheriff talks to Doc and Red.
Sheriff says, "If a tornado hits, folks will need our help."

police officer

Sheriff is a police officer.
He keeps everyone safe.

doctor

Doc is the town doctor.
He keeps everyone healthy.

firefighter

Red is a firefighter.
He puts out fires.

© Disney/Pixar, Hudson Hornet™, Mercury™

Let's Match Words

Who are the helpers in Radiator Springs?
Draw a line from the word to the correct picture.

police officer   **doctor**   **firefighter**

Draw a picture of someone who helps you.

© Disney/Pixar, Hudson Hornet™, Mercury™

Let's Understand Word Meanings

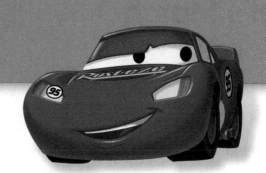

Read each sentence.
Put a ✔ under **Yes** or **No**.

	Yes	No
1. A doctor like helps people.	☐	☐
2. A firefighter like moves slow.	☐	☐
3. A police officer like flies in a rocket.	☐	☐

Draw a picture of yourself as a firefighter.

© Disney/Pixar. Hudson Hornet™, Mercury™

Let's Sort Words

Read each word.
Count the letters in each word.
Write the words in the chart.

up	his	I	he

1 letter	2 letters	3 letters

Write the missing word. Use a word from the chart.

went _____ to take a look.

© Disney/Pixar. Mercury™

Let's Write Words

Read the words.
Write the missing word to complete each sentence.

It	We	for	If

1. " _____ _____ will see if the  will come!"

says _____ .

2. " _____ _____ might miss us!" says _____ .

3. "We will watch _____ _____ the  !"

says _____ .

4. " _____ _____ it comes, I'll be ready!" says  .

© Disney/Pixar, Hudson Hornet™, Mercury™

Let's Find Things That Don't Go Together

Look at the pictures.
Circle the picture
that does not belong.

 **firefighter**

 **red light**

 **race flag**

 **medicine**

 **rocks**

 **doctor**

 **siren**

 **police officer**

 **cactus**

© Disney/Pixar, Hudson Hornet™, Jeep®; Sarge's rank insignia used with the approval of the U.S. Army, Mercury™

Al Oft goes up for another look at the weather. Soon he's back. "The tornado passed us by!" he shouts. "Radiator Springs is safe!"

"Woo-hoo!" Lightning cheers. "We can have the car rally after all!"

Everyone cheers! But the cars have gotten so dusty, they can't see their colors! Red volunteers to wash them, and soon they look like new.

Can you read the color words?

blue

red

green

yellow

purple

black

44

© Disney/Pixar, Chevrolet®, Fiat™, Model T™, Porsche®

Let's Learn Words for Colors

Read the words.
Color the cars the correct color.

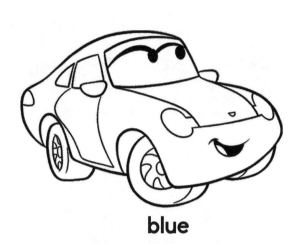

blue

yellow

red

purple

green

black

© Disney/Pixar. Chevrolet®, Fiat™, Model T™, Porsche®

Let's Write Words

Read the words.
Write the correct color word under each car.

| red | black | yellow | blue | green | purple |

colors

_____

_ _ _ _ _ _ _ _ _ _ _ _ _ _ _ _

_____

© Disney/Pixar, Chevrolet®, Fiat™, Model T™, Porsche®

Let's Sort Words

Read each word.
Count the letters in each word.
Write the words in the chart.

him	me	with	you

2 letters	3 letters	4 letters
_____	_____	_____
_____	_____	_____
_____	_____	_____
_____	_____	_____

Write the missing word. Use a word from the chart.

washes the cars _____ his hose.

© Disney/Pixar, Porsche®

Let's Write Words

Read the words.
Write the missing word to complete each sentence.

| saw | out | be | at |

1. Maybe the  will come _____.

2. The  looked _____ the sky.

3. They _____ the  !

4. The  were happy to _____ safe!

48

© Disney/Pixar. Fiat™, Jeep®, Mercury™

Let's Find Words

Help Red get to the dusty car.
Follow the color words.

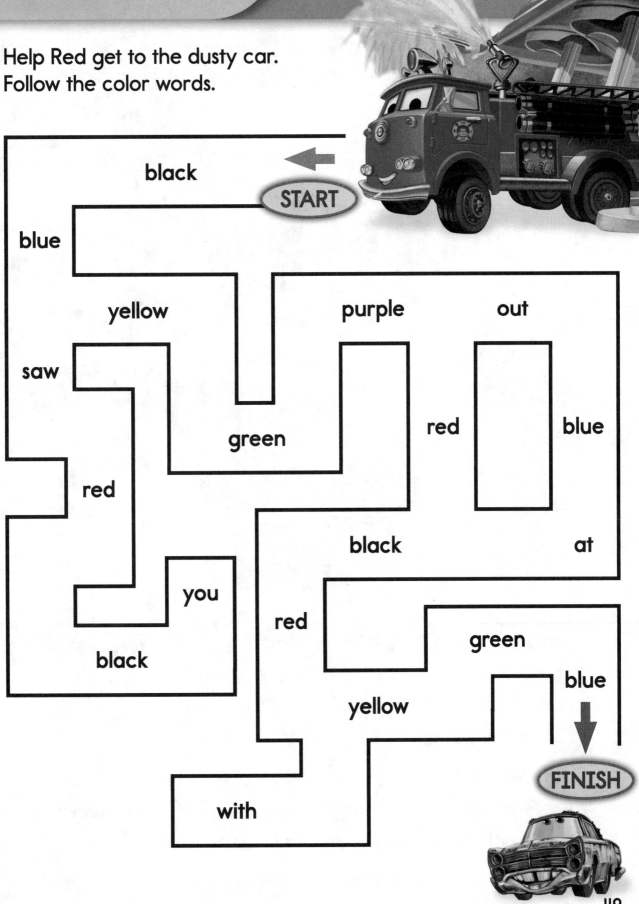

black

START

blue

yellow   purple   out

saw

red   blue

green

red

black   at

red

you

green

black

blue

yellow

FINISH

with

© Disney/Pixar

tall stack

Guido is putting tires into tall stacks
and short stacks. Cars from all over the
country come to town and make their way
to Luigi's tire shop.

"*Mama mia!*" Luigi cries. "Do all of these cars need
new tires?" His big headlights and little fog lights flash
on and off as he takes care of his customers.

Radiator Springs is a very busy place!

© Disney/Pixar, Model T™

short stack

big light

little light

© Disney/Pixar, Fiat™, Model T™

Let's Match Words

Read each size word.
Find the matching sticker
on page 81.

little

big

size

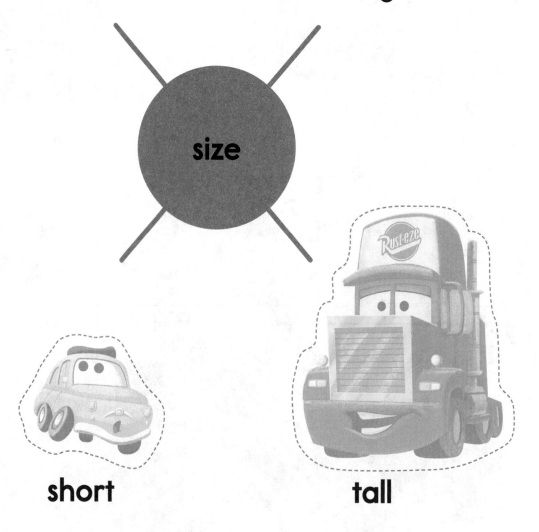

short

tall

52

© Disney/Pixar, Fiat™, Mack®, Model T™

Let's Sort Words

Read each word.
Count the letters in each word.
Write the words in the chart.

| had | an | she | her |

2 letters	3 letters

Write the missing word. Use a word from the chart.

The  _____ a long way to go.

© Disney/Pixar, Mack®

Let's Write Words

Read the words.
Write the missing word to
complete each sentence.

| Then | my | your | This |

1. "Do you like _____ ?" asks the ____.

2. "I like _____ !" says the ____.

3. _____ the ____ go to Radiator Springs.

4. "_____ is fun!" say the ____.

© Disney/Pixar

Let's Find Words

Help the cars get to Radiator Springs.
Follow the size words.

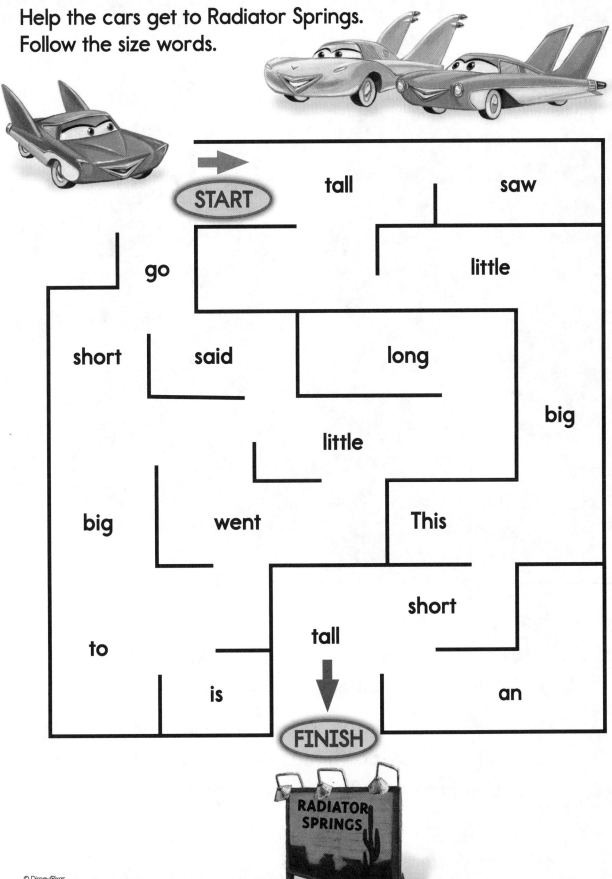

© Disney/Pixar

That night, Lightning welcomes the visiting cars to town. "Welcome to Radiator Springs!" he says. "Thank you all for coming. Let the rally begin!"

The cars from Radiator Springs start off the car rally with a cruise down Main Street. The other cars soon join them. They make a grand parade!

All the cars cheer and shout, "We love Radiator Springs!"

© Disney/Pixar. Chevrolet®, Fiat™, Hudson Hornet™, Jeep®, Porsche®. ©Volkswagen AG

© Disney/Pixar

Chevrolet®, Fiat™, Hudson Hornet™, Jeep®, Mercury™, Porsche®, ©Volkswagen AG

Race to Win!

START

START

saw

one

their

were

with

him

he

you

be

out

went

were

came

their

came

got

is

to

58

© Disney/Pixar. Mercury™, Model T™, Porsche®

1

Lose a Turn

Spin Again

2

FINISH

FINISH

was

to

out

you

me

got

if

for

I

went

saw

it

up

was

him

at

59

Race to Win!
A game for two to four players

Setup

- Have an adult cut out two of the game pieces on page 61, following the pink lines. Fold each game piece on the blue line so it stands upright.
- Each player chooses a game piece and a track and places his or her game piece on START.
- Decide which player will go first.

Spinner Assembly

- You will need a paper clip and a pencil to use the spinner.
- Put the pencil point through one end of the paper clip and place the pencil point on the ☆ found on the spinner.

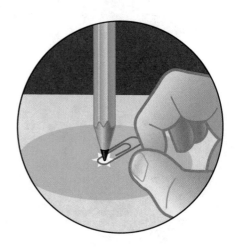

- To spin, players flick the paper clip while holding the pencil steady.
- The paper-clip end not held by the pencil will point like an arrow.

Play Race to Win!

- Player spins and moves his or her game piece the number of spaces shown on the spinner.
- Player reads the word on the space where he or she lands. If the player cannot read the word, another player can help by reading the word for that player.
- It is now the next player's turn.
- The first player to reach the finish space is the winner.

Special Spaces on the Spinner

- If a player spins LOSE A TURN, that player loses a turn and does not move his or her game piece.

- If a player spins SPIN AGAIN, that player spins again.

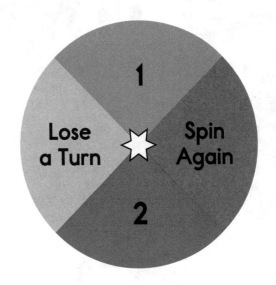

Game pieces for Race to Win!

© Disney/Pixar
© Disney/Pixar; Hudson Hornet™
© Disney/Pixar; Plymouth Superbird™; Petty®
© Disney/Pixar

© Disney/Pixar. Fiat™, Hudson Hornet™, Model T™, Porsche®

an	she	her	had
my	your	then	this
is	go	was	to
went	I	saw	said
me	came	in	you

an	she	her	had
my	your	then	this
is	go	was	to
went	I	saw	said
me	came	in	you

Go Fish!

A game for two to three players

Set Up

- Have an adult cut out the flash cards from pages 63 and 65.

- Decide who will be the dealer and which player will go first.

- Dealer mixes up the cards and gives six cards to each player.

- Dealer places remaining flash cards in a pile facedown on the playing surface.

Play Go Fish!

- Players look at their cards to see if they have any that match. Then they place their matched pairs on the playing surface in front of them.

- The first player looks at the cards in his or her hand and asks the second player if he or she has a flash card that matches one of the cards the first player is asking for.

- If the second player is holding a flash card that matches what the first player is asking for, that player must give up his or her card to the first player.

- If the second player does not have a card that matches what the first player is asking for, that second player says, "Go fish!" The first player then selects one card from the draw pile and places it in his or her hand. It is now the next player's turn.

- Play continues until all cards have been played. The player with the highest number of matched pairs is the winner.

Answer Keys

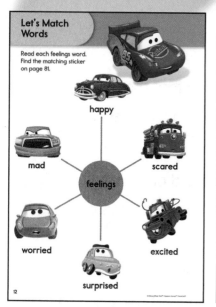

Let's Match Words

Read each feelings word. Find the matching sticker on page 81.

- happy
- scared
- excited
- surprised
- worried
- mad

feelings

Let's Sort Words

Read each word. Count the letters in each word. Write the words in the chart.

said	so	but	is

2 letters	3 letters	4 letters
so	but	said
is		

Write the missing word. Use a word from the chart.

_____is_____ happy.

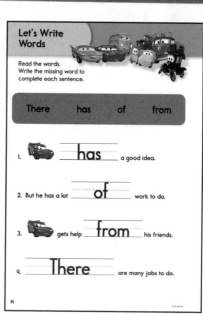

Let's Write Words

Read the words. Write the missing word to complete each sentence.

There	has	of	from

1. _____has_____ a good idea.

2. But he has a lot _____of_____ work to do.

3. _____ gets help _____from_____ his friends.

4. _____There_____ are many jobs to do.

Let's Review Word Meanings

Look at each car. Circle the word that tells how the car feels.

- sad / (happy)
- (excited) / sad
- happy / (mad)

Draw how you feel when you get a new toy.

Answers will vary.

15

Let's Review Words for Days of the Week

Look at Lightning's calendar.

Sunday	Monday	Tuesday
Pave.	Wash.	Clean.

Wednesday	Thursday	Friday	Saturday
Point.	Get tires.	Get gas.	Make signs.

Circle the correct day of the week.

- Sunday / (Monday)
- (Tuesday) / Thursday
- (Friday) / Saturday
- Monday / (Wednesday)

18

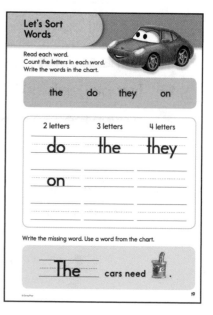

Let's Sort Words

Read each word. Count the letters in each word. Write the words in the chart.

the	do	they	on

2 letters	3 letters	4 letters
do	the	they
on		

Write the missing word. Use a word from the chart.

_____The_____ cars need _____ .

19

© Disney/Pixar, Chevrolet®, Fiat™, Hudson Hornet™, Jeep®, Mack®, Mercury™, Model T™, Porsche®, ©Volkswagen AG

Let's Write Words

Read the words.
Write the missing word to complete each sentence.

and	That	All	have

1. The ____ **have** ____ so much work!

2. **All** ____ the ____ work.

3. The ____ clean ____ **and** ____ clean.

4. **That** ____ is not clean.

20

Let's Find Words

Help Sally find Lightning.
Follow the words for the days of the week.

21

Let's Match Words

Read each question.
Find the correct answer sticker on page 81.

1. Who works in a store?
_____

2. Who works on the street?
_____

3. Who works in a firehouse?

Draw something you buy in a food store.

Answers will vary.

24

Let's Write Words

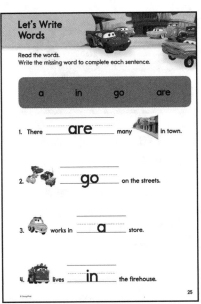

Read the words.
Write the missing word to complete each sentence.

a	in	go	are

1. There ____ **are** ____ many ____ in town.

2. ____ **go** ____ on the streets.

3. ____ works in ____ **a** ____ store.

4. ____ lives ____ **in** ____ the firehouse.

25

Let's Sort Words

Look at the pictures and words.
Write the words in the chart.

fire hose   oil cans   tires   firefighter

Things you see in a store	Things you see in a firehouse
oil cans	**fire hose**
tires	**firefighter**

Draw a picture of your favorite store.

Answers will vary.

26

Let's Review Word Meanings

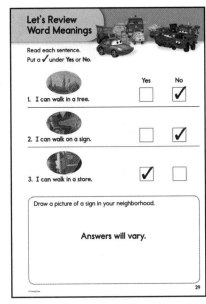

Read each sentence.
Put a ✓ under **Yes** or **No**.

	Yes	No
1. I can walk in a tree.		✓
2. I can walk on a sign.		✓
3. I can walk in a store.	✓	

Draw a picture of a sign in your neighborhood.

Answers will vary.

29

Let's Match Words

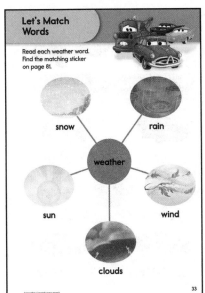

Read each weather word.
Find the matching sticker on page 81.

snow   rain   weather   sun   wind   clouds

33

Let's Sort Words

Look at the pictures and words.
Write the words in the chart

water   hat   sunglasses   earmuffs

Things cars need on a snowy day.	Things cars need on a sunny day.
hat	**water**
earmuffs	**sunglasses**

Draw a picture of yourself on a rainy day.

Answers will vary.

34

Let's Sort Words

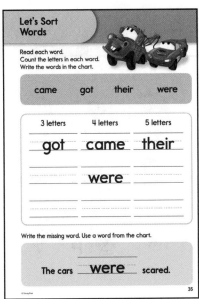

Read each word.
Count the letters in each word.
Write the words in the chart.

came	got	their	were

3 letters	4 letters	5 letters
got	**came**	**their**
	were	

Write the missing word. Use a word from the chart.

The cars ____ **were** ____ scared.

35

© Disney/Pixar, Chevrolet®, Fiat™, Hudson Hornet™, Jeep®, Mack®, Mercury™, Model T™, Porsche®, ©Volkswagen AG

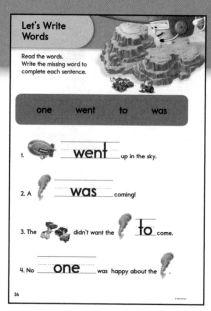

Let's Write Words

Read the words.
Write the missing word to complete each sentence.

one	went	to	was

1. ___went___ up in the sky.

2. A ___was___ coming!

3. The ___ didn't want the ___to___ come.

4. No ___one___ was happy about the ___.

36

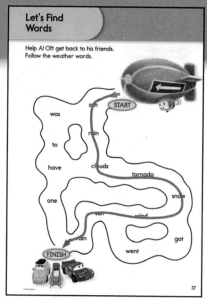

Let's Find Words

Help Al Oft get back to his friends.
Follow the weather words.

START

was · sun
rain
to
have · clouds
one · tornado
sun · snow
rain · wind
FINISH · went · got

37

Let's Match Words

Who are the helpers in Radiator Springs?
Draw a line from the word to the correct picture.

police officer   doctor   firefighter

Draw a picture of someone who helps you.

Answers will vary.

39

Let's Understand Word Meanings

Read each sentence.
Put a ✓ under Yes or No.

	Yes	No
1. A doctor like ___ helps people.	✓	
2. A firefighter like ___ moves slow.		✓
3. A police officer like ___ flies in a rocket.		✓

Draw a picture of yourself as a firefighter.

Answers will vary.

40

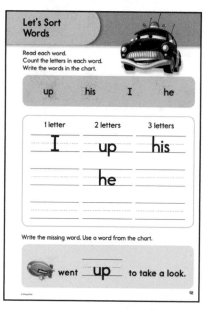

Let's Sort Words

Read each word.
Count the letters in each word.
Write the words in the chart.

up	his	I	he

1 letter	2 letters	3 letters
I	up	his
	he	

Write the missing word. Use a word from the chart.

___ went ___up___ to take a look.

41

Let's Write Words

Read the words.
Write the missing word to complete each sentence.

It	We	for	If

1. "___We___ will see if the ___ will come!" says ___.

2. "___It___ might miss us!" says ___.

3. "We will watch ___for___ the ___!" says ___.

4. "___If___ it comes, I'll be ready!" says ___.

42

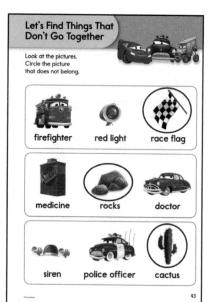

Let's Find Things That Don't Go Together

Look at the pictures.
Circle the picture that does not belong.

firefighter	red light	race flag
medicine	rocks	doctor
siren	police officer	cactus

43

Let's Learn Words for Colors

Read the words.
Color the cars the correct color.

blue   yellow
red   purple
green   black

45

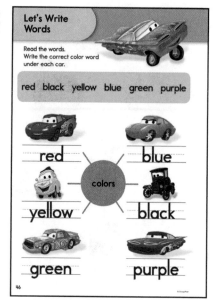

Let's Write Words

Read the words.
Write the correct color word under each car.

red	black	yellow	blue	green	purple

red   blue
colors
yellow   black
green   purple

46

70

© Disney/Pixar. Chevrolet®, Fiat™, Hudson Hornet™, Jeep®, Mack®, Mercury™, Model T™, Porsche®, ©Volkswagen AG

Let's Sort Words

Read each word.
Count the letters in each word.
Write the words in the chart.

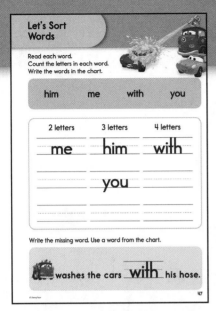

| him | me | with | you |

2 letters	3 letters	4 letters
me	him	with
	you	

Write the missing word. Use a word from the chart.

with washes the cars **with** his hose.

47

Let's Write Words

Read the words.
Write the missing word to complete each sentence.

| saw | out | be | at |

1. Maybe the will come **out**.

2. The looked **at** the sky.

3. They **saw** the !

4. The were happy to **be** safe!

48

Let's Find Words

Help Red get to the dusty car.
Follow the color words.

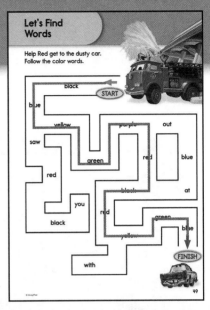

START — black
blue
yellow — purple — out
saw
green — red — blue
red
black
you — red — at
black
green — blue
yellow
with
FINISH

49

Let's Match Words

Read each size word.
Find the matching sticker on page 82.

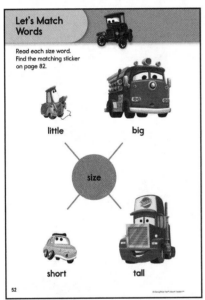

little   big

size

short   tall

52

Let's Sort Words

Read each word.
Count the letters in each word.
Write the words in the chart.

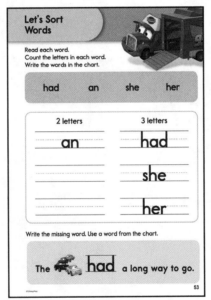

| had | an | she | her |

2 letters	3 letters
an	had
	she
	her

Write the missing word. Use a word from the chart.

The **had** a long way to go.

53

Let's Write Words

Read the words.
Write the missing word to complete each sentence.

| Then | my | your | This |

1. "Do you like **my** ?" asks the .

2. "I like **your** !" says the .

3. **Then** the go to Radiator Springs.

4. **This** is fun!" say the .

54

Let's Find Words

Help the cars get to Radiator Springs.
Follow the size words.

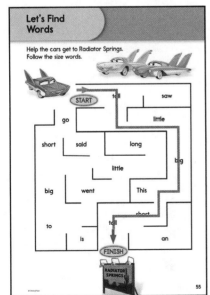

START — tall   saw
go   little
short   said   long
                big
little
big   went   This
short
to   tall   an
is
FINISH
RADIATOR SPRINGS

55

© Disney/Pixar, Chevrolet®, Fiat™, Hudson Hornet™, Jeep®, Mack®, Mercury™, Model T™, Porsche®, ©Volkswagen AG

Here are all the new words I can read and write.

© Disney/Pixar

I can read and write these words...

a	○	got	○	me	○	then	○
all	○	had	○	my	○	there	○
an	○	has	○	of	○	they	○
and	○	have	○	on	○	this	○
are	○	he	○	one	○	to	○
at	○	her	○	out	○	up	○
be	○	him	○	said	○	was	○
but	○	his	○	saw	○	we	○
came	○	I	○	she	○	went	○
do	○	if	○	so	○	were	○
for	○	in	○	that	○	with	○
from	○	is	○	the	○	you	○
go	○	it	○	their	○	your	○

© Disney/Pixar

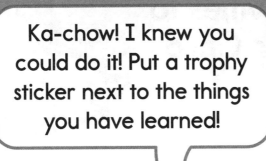

Ka-chow! I knew you could do it! Put a trophy sticker next to the things you have learned!

I can name words for...

THINGS IN A NEIGHBORHOOD
firehouse
sidewalk
sign
store
street
tree

NEIGHBORHOOD HELPERS
doctor
firefighter
police officer

DAYS OF THE WEEK
Sunday
Monday
Tuesday
Wednesday
Thursday
Friday
Saturday

FEELINGS
excited
happy
mad
sad
scared
surprised
worried

WEATHER
clouds
rain
snow
sun
tornado
wind

COLORS
black
blue
green
purple
red
yellow

© Disney/Pixar, Mack®

Additional Activities to Share with Your Child

How does your child learn?

Research shows that all children benefit from a wide range of learning activities. Here are a few exercises to do together to strengthen your child's vocabulary and word-recognition skills.

Search for sight words.

• Be on the lookout for sight words around the house. Point to letters your child knows. Count the letters in each word.

Read sight words every day.

• Help your child develop quick and automatic recognition of the most common words. Schedule one night a week to listen to your child read a set of sight-word cards. Begin with five words and slowly build up to fifty words. Ask your child to read the words in silly ways—using a soft voice, a monster voice, a fast or slow voice. Or, read the words with va-room, va-room car sounds! Make learning words fun!

Play word games.

• Use sight-word cards to play games such Bingo or Blackout. Make a set of reusable game boards by drawing 3 x 3 grids on paper (with a total of nine squares on each). Write a word in each square. Use buttons, cereal circles, or bow-shaped pasta for markers. Take turns reading the word cards. Look at your game boards to see if the same word can be covered more than one time. For Bingo, be the first player to cover words in

© Disney/Pixar, Model T™, Porsche®

rows going across, up and down, or diagonally. For Blackout, be the first player to cover the entire board.

Practice sight words anywhere.

• The next time you eat out, use the paper tablecloth to practice sight words with your child. Write a word, then have your child use the word in a sentence to tell about something he or she sees in the restaurant or on the menu. For example:

and   I want vanilla **and** chocolate ice cream.

has   The waiter **has** a pen.

Make sentence puzzles.

• On a strip of paper, write a sentence that describes a place, person, or thing from your neighborhood. Cut the sentence up into words. Have your child put the sentence back together. Help your child read the sentence to make sure the words are in the right order. For example:

Sight words: I, go, to, the, for

I go to the café for breakfast.

© Disney/Pixar

Practice reading color words.

• Write a color word on an index card. Have your child read the word and then find three things around your home that are that color. Then have your child draw or write the names of the objects he or she found on the back of the index card.

Make a days-of-the-week wall hanging.

• Using seven different colors of construction paper, cut one three-inch strip for each day. Glue the strips vertically on a piece of cardboard. Help your child write the days of the week in order at the top. (Write one day in each color strip.)

Tie a piece of string on each corner of the top to hang up the chart.

Have your child tell you things he or she does on each day. Use stickers or draw pictures to illustrate each of these activities.

Put a clothespin on the top of the chart, and have your child move the clothespin to keep track of the days of the week.

© Disney/Pixar, Chevrolet®, Porsche®

Name one more.

- As you take walks around your neighborhood, ask your child to name words that fit a particular category. As you walk past the playground, for example, ask your child to name two things you would find at a playground. Then ask your child to name one more. Help your child see how these words go together because they are all things you can find at a playground.

© Disney/Pixar; Fiat™; Model T™

My Favorite Words

1. Look at the example.
2. Draw a picture of something you love to do.
3. Write a list of words that go with your picture.

Fishing

worm
net
fish
hook
pole
sinker
catch
water
bobber

Draw your picture here.

Write your
word list here

_____

_____

_____

_____

_____

_____

_____

© Disney/Pixar, Chevrolet®, Hudson Hornet™

Ka-chow! You did it!

CONGRATULATIONS!

_____

(Name)

has completed the School Skills Workbook:

LET'S LEARN SIGHT WORDS AND VOCABULARY

Presented on

_____

(Date)

_____

(Parent's Signature)

© Disney/Pixar. Porsche®

Porsche®

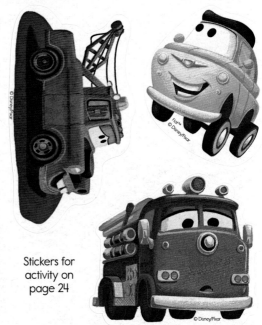

© Disney/Pixar

Figre™

© Disney/Pixar

Hudson Hornet™

Figre

© Disney/Pixar

© Disney/Pixar

Stickers for activity on page 12

© Disney/Pixar

Stickers for activity on page 24

© Disney/Pixar

© Disney/Pixar

© Disney/Pixar

Stickers for activity on page 33

Stickers for activity on page 52

Figre™

© Disney/Pixar

© Disney/Pixar

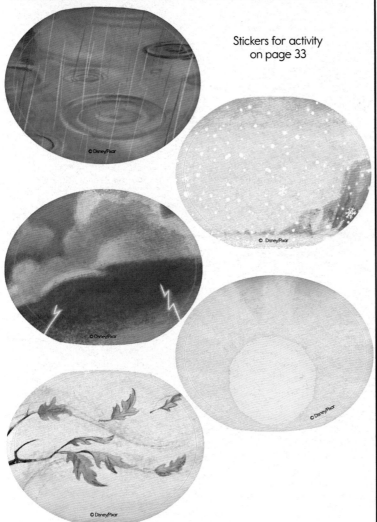

© Disney/Pixar

© Disney/Pixar

© Disney/Pixar

© Disney/Pixar

© Disney/Pixar. Mack®

Rust-eze

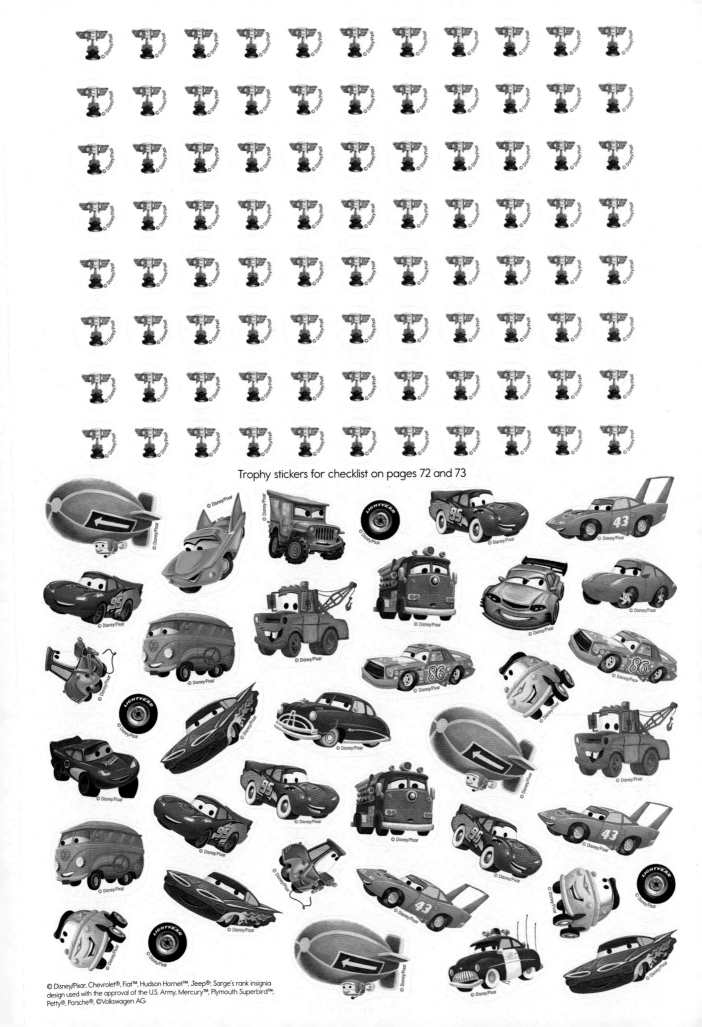

Trophy stickers for checklist on pages 72 and 73

© Disney/Pixar, Chevrolet®, Fiat™, Hudson Hornet™, Jeep®; Sarge's rank insignia design used with the approval of the U.S. Army, Mercury™, Plymouth Superbird™; Petty®, Porsche®, ©Volkswagen AG